Sarah –
I will be so
to hear about
chooses to be your .
May you experience
"immeasurably more" of Jesus
with each step of your
mentoring journey!
Nancy ♡

TOGETHER

come. be. move.

BOOK ONE

ISBN-13:978-1976323508

ISBN-10:1976323509

And let us not give up meeting together. Some are in the habit of doing this. Instead, let us encourage one another with words of hope. Let us do this even more as you see Christ's return approaching.

– Hebrews 10:25 NIrV

TABLE OF
CONTENTS

Two are better than one, because they have a good return for their labor: If either of them falls down, one can help the other up. But pity anyone who falls and has no one to help them up.

- Ecclesiastes 4:9-10

FROM MY HEART TO YOURS

Life is hard. It's messy. I have issues. You have issues. We need each other. We're made that way – our hearts are designed to connect with others. In life, our journey will have unexpected twists and turns, sometimes that leave us on shaky ground. We can feel stuck, in a rut, and unable to move. And the enemy of our souls wants us there. He especially wants us to feel alone.

But what if we had someone to walk with, someone who is a little further down the path? Someone who has been there and who understands. Someone who loves, listens, encourages and prays. Someone who is unshaken because they know their God and want others to know Him, too.

I'm so glad you have this book in your hands because it means you don't want to journey alone. Mentoring is one of the best ways we can experience the fullness of life that God desires for us. He has made us for community. He knows the strength, joy, and peace it will bring to our lives. Our Father wants us to experience the joy of coming together, being connected and moving into closer relationship with others and with Him.

As I wrote this guide, three words consistently resonated in my mind and heart. They are simple words – Come. Be. Move.

We need to **come** together – to be intentional, to be available, to give our time and our genuine presence to one another. God will do beautiful things in the lives of those who are teachable and sincere in their desire to grow closer to Him.

We need to **be** together – united in purpose and growing into the fullness of who God has made us to be, each with our own unique story, life experiences, personality, and giftings.

We need to **move** together – in the direction of God's best plans for us. Movement is what gives us hope that God is able to do more than we can ask or imagine. We move together when we pray together and ask God to step into every aspect of our lives.

I'm so thankful you have taken the important first step of connecting with someone through mentoring. Whether you are a mentor or a mentee, I pray that God will use this guide as a tool to help you experience true, life-changing discipleship. I also sincerely hope and pray that it multiplies – like ripples on a pond, far reaching into the lives of many more.

My heartfelt prayer for you . . .

> *May the God of hope fill you with all joy and peace as you trust in him,*
> *so that you may overflow with hope by the power of the Holy Spirit.*
> – Romans 15:13

– NANCY LINDGREN
Founder, MORE Mentoring

Whoever refreshes others

will be refreshed.

– Proverbs 11:25b

A NOTE TO **MENTORS**

I remember the first time a young mom asked me to be her mentor. The word "mentor" alone caused me some slight panic! It sounded so formal— like I had to have all the answers and my life put together, as well as be an advisor, teacher, counselor, and Bible scholar. Well, she and I quickly realized that was not what she was looking for nor was it who I was. She simply wanted someone to connect with, someone willing to walk alongside her in her journey. So, we started meeting together. I loved her, listened to her, and encouraged her. Then we would pray together over all the things that were heavy on her heart for that day. As our friendship grew, we watched God answer prayer after prayer in the most creative and miraculous ways. Together, we grew in awe of our great God. My hope is that through mentoring, you also will experience the refreshing fullness that comes from pouring into others.

The ministry of MORE Mentoring defines a mentor this way:

"Someone with a little more experience who comes alongside another and points her to Jesus."

WHAT IS A MENTEE LOOKING FOR IN A MENTOR?

Time – The biggest need a mentee has is for her mentor to be available.

Trust – She needs to know she can share the hard things with you and that confidentiality is a priority.

Truth – Your mentee wants to know the truth from God's Word. She also wants you to be honest with her and speak truth over her life.

Tenderness – She desperately needs your empathy, love and acceptance.

Togetherness – She wants to be with you. Consider doing fun things together beyond the mentoring sessions. Invite her to go shopping, to a movie or do a service project together.

A NOTE TO **MENTEES**

It took me six years to gain enough courage to ask the woman who is now my mentor if she would be willing to mentor me. We live in different states. She's incredibly busy. And I was sure she had countless other women asking her to be their mentor since she is the founder of a large prayer ministry. In reality, she was honored to be asked. We keep things simple. We share life updates. I ask her questions. She doesn't just give me answers but shares her story and lessons learned. She speaks truth with grace, leads me to Scripture, and points me to Jesus. We are always intentional about prayer and that brings the greatest encouragement of all. She shares with me out of the overflow of what God has poured into her. In return, then I feel empowered and inspired to pour into others. We both come away refreshed. My hope for you is that your mentoring experience will be an abundantly refreshing time as well.

The ministry of MORE Mentoring defines a mentee this way:

"Someone who desires to grow in faith by being teachable and eager to learn from a more experienced follower of Christ."

WHAT IS A MENTOR LOOKING FOR IN A MENTEE?

Action – Take the first step. Be the initiator. Oftentimes a mentor doesn't see herself as one. It's always an honor to be asked.

Authenticity – Be real. Be vulnerable. Share your struggles. Share your joys.

Ask – Ask your mentor good questions. Ask her to pray for specific requests. Ask her for help when you need it.

Aware – Be aware of your mentor's boundaries (her time and commitments, etc.). Don't expect more of her than what she has to give.

Appreciation – Your mentor is making an investment in you. It's so good for her to hear how her life is making a difference in yours.

HOW TO USE THIS GUIDE

This book is both a hands-on guide and a personal journal. It is divided into 12 sessions that lead mentors and mentees through Conversation Starters, Encouragement Starters and Prayer Starters. At the end of each section, there is a place for journaling to record notes, ideas, lessons learned, key verses or written prayers. The hope is that this will serve not only as a helpful tool during mentoring but also as a beautiful reminder of how far you've come along the way.

CONVERSATION STARTERS

Each session contains four Conversation Starters — the first two are fun and lighthearted while the other two are designed to prompt deeper, faith-building conversation. You can choose one or two questions or talk through all four. It's up to you. Remember, these are just to get the conversation started. More than likely, you'll discover that as you get to know one another, your conversation will unfold more naturally each time you meet.

ENCOURAGEMENT STARTERS

Everyone loves to be encouraged. For some, offering encouragement comes very naturally. But for others, it's quite challenging. These Encouragement Starters are designed to equip mentors and mentees with meaningful ways to encourage one another through offering support, instilling confidence, and nurturing hope. They will help you develop this valuable skill of blessing others with encouragement – sharing a verse of Scripture, speaking truth over someone, or recognizing praiseworthy qualities in her life.

PRAYER STARTERS

Prayer is such a beautiful and important part of the mentoring experience. It's where our burdens are lifted as our focus shifts from our circumstances to our great God. When our hearts unite with another and we agree in faith for God's best plan, it changes us. We move from fear to trust, from worry to rest, from doubt to hope, and from anxiety to peace. It ultimately moves us to grow closer to the Lord and to others. Prayer is just as much about listening as it is talking. The Lord wants to speak to us. Take time to let Him do that.

The Prayer Starters in each session provide direction and inspiration for being intentional about prayer. It's important to remember that prayer is not about saying the "right words." It is the posture of your heart - the "eyes of your heart" - that draw you into sweeter intimacy and a deeper relationship with the Lord.

I keep asking that the God of our Lord Jesus Christ, the glorious Father, may give you the Spirit of wisdom and revelation, so that you may know him better. I pray that the eyes of your heart may be enlightened in order that you may know the hope to which he has called you. – Ephesians 1:17-18a

Prayer Starters will direct the eyes of our hearts to:

Look Up – Look at God. Praise Him for who He is. Look at the heart of God. Look at His attributes and His character. When we start with a focus on God, He becomes greater and our circumstances become much smaller. Praise also defeats the enemy.

Look Within – Look inward asking God to reveal your sin – the places that need to be cleansed. Only when we empty ourselves of "self" can we receive all that the Spirit has for us. Confession then frees us to move forward in repentance and become all God has created us to be.

Look Around – Look around for the countless ways God has surrounded you with evidence of His presence, provision, and protection. Look at the hands of God. Express gratitude for the specific ways He has blessed you. Thank Him for being attentive to your prayers and for His promise to answer according to His will.

Look To Him – Look to Jesus as He is standing before you saying, "What do you want me to do for you?" He wants us to ask Him. Use His Word. Personalize Scripture by inserting a name (even your own) as you pray. Be specific. Believe Him. Your faith is what pleases God and moves Him to action.

GETTING TO
KNOW YOU

Mentor's/Mentee's Name: _____

Contact information (indicate preferred method of communicating):

Phone _____

Email _____

Address _____

_____

Who are the important people in your life? (family members, close friends, neighbors, etc.):

_____

_____

_____

What is your background story? (Where are you from? Where did you grow up? What was your childhood like? Where did you go to school? How long have you lived here? etc.):

_____

_____

_____

_____

What is your occupation or current job? _____

_____

How do you spend your free time? _____

_____

_____

Where and how are you involved in others' lives? (church, community, etc.)

_____

_____

What is your faith story? _____

_____

_____

_____

What are some of your favorite things? (ie. The color yellow, coffee, sitting on my back porch, anything chocolate, sunshine, etc.):

_____

_____

Any other special things to note: _____

_____

Best days/time/place to meet: _____

SESSION
ONE

SESSION 1

DATE_____

CONVERSATION STARTERS

What was your favorite thing to pretend when you were a child?

If you could pick a day to spend with your family, what would that look like?

What has been a significant spiritual experience in your life? Why?

What is one tangible way you would like to grow in your faith?

ENCOURAGEMENT STARTERS

Mentors, select and share a verse that would encourage your mentee today.

Mentees, if you could ask your mentor one question today, what would it be?

PRAYER STARTERS

How can I pray for you today?

Look Up – Lord, I praise You for being FAITHFUL.

Your kingdom is an everlasting kingdom, and your dominion endures through all generations. The LORD is trustworthy in all he promises and faithful in all he does. – Psalm 145:13

Yet this I call to mind and therefore I have hope: Because of the LORD's great love we are not consumed, for his compassions never fail. They are new every morning; great is your faithfulness. – Lamentations 3:21-23

God, I love that You are ...

Look Within – Lord, show me which fruit of the Spirit I'm not producing (love, joy, peace, patience, kindness, goodness, faithfulness, gentleness or self-control?):

Look Around – Thank you, Lord for these specific ways you have shown me your goodness and answered my prayers (in the past or recently):

Look to Him – Father, these are the specific things I am trusting you for:

Teach me your way, LORD, that I may rely on your faithfulness; give me an undivided heart, that I may fear your name. – Psalm 86:11

No temptation has overtaken _____ *except what is common to mankind. And God is faithful; he will not let* _____ *be tempted beyond what he/she can bear. But when* _____ *is tempted, he will also provide a way out so that he/she can endure it.* – 1 Corinthians 10:13

Now, take time to listen to the Lord.

Ask Him – Lord, what do You want me to know? What verse of Scripture do you want me to meditate on and hide in my heart?

Lord, I praise You for being so faithful and loving to me.
Forgive me for not consistently being faithful to You.
Thank You for the many ways You are working in my life.
I ask You for a faithful, undivided heart that I might fear Your name. Amen.

∾

REFLECTIONS

_____

_____

_____

_____

_____

_____

_____

_____

_____

_____

_____

_____

_____

_____

_____

_____

_____

_____

_____

_____

_____

_____

SESSION
TWO

SESSION 2

CONVERSATION STARTERS

What is your favorite movie? Why?

What was a success you had this past week?

When do you feel the most valuable?

What are some characteristics you have heard taught about God that are difficult to grasp?

ENCOURAGEMENT STARTERS

Mentors, share a story of a time in your life that was really hard but how you saw God bring beauty out of it.

Mentees, if you could ask your mentor one question today, what would it be?

PRAYER STARTERS

How can I pray for you today?

Look Up – Lord, I praise You for being POWERFUL.

To God belong wisdom and power; counsel and understanding are his. – Job 12:13

For since the creation of the world God's invisible qualities – his eternal power and divine nature – have been clearly seen, being understood from what has been made, so that people are without excuse. – Romans 1:20

Father, the quality or attribute I appreciate about You is ...

Look Within – Lord, show me if (and where) I may be living in a spirit of fear rather than power, love and self-control.

Look Around – Thank you, Lord for these specific ways you have shown me your power and answered my prayers (in the past or recently):

Look to Him – Father, these are the specific things I am trusting you for:

The prayer of a righteous person is powerful and effective. – James 5:16b

For the Spirit God gave _____ does not make him/her timid but gives him/her power, love and self-discipline. – 2 Timothy 1:7

Now, take time to listen to the Lord.

Ask Him – What do You want me to hear from you today? How do you want me to move towards You?

Father, I love that You are all-powerful and there is nothing too hard for You.
I confess my desire to be in control.
Thank You for giving me a spirit of power, love and self-control.
I ask for a prayer life that is powerful and effective. Amen.

∽

REFLECTIONS

_____

_____

_____

_____

_____

_____

_____

_____

_____

_____

_____

_____

_____

_____

_____

_____

_____

_____

_____

_____

_____

_____

SESSION
THREE

SESSION 3

DATE_____

CONVERSATION STARTERS

If you could travel to any country, where would you choose to go? Why?

When was the last time you laughed so hard you cried?

How would you complete this statement? I feel loved when ...

To you, what is the most precious thing about Jesus?

ENCOURAGEMENT STARTERS

Mentors, share a quality that you see in in your mentee that is like Jesus.

Mentees, if you could ask your mentor one question today, what would it be?

PRAYER STARTERS

How can I pray for you today?

Look Up – Lord, I praise You for being LOVING.

All the ways of the LORD are loving and faithful toward those who keep the demands of his covenant. – Psalm 25:10

How priceless is your unfailing love, O God! People take refuge in the shadow of your wings. – Psalm 36:7

Lord, I exalt You for being ...

Look Within – Lord, show me the relationships in my life where I haven't been very loving. Am I impatient, unkind, envious, boastful, proud, rude, self-seeking, easily angered, keeping a record of wrongs? Do I always protect, trust, hope and persevere? (1 Corinthians 13:4-7)

Look Around – Thank you, Lord, for these specific ways you have shown me your love and answered my prayers (recently or in the past):

Look to Him – Father, these are the specific things I am asking and trusting you for:

Knowledge puffs up, but love builds up. – 1 Corinthians 8:1b

The LORD your God is with _____, the Mighty Warrior who saves. He will take great delight in _____, in his love he will no longer rebuke you, but will rejoice over you with singing. – Zephaniah 3:17

Now, take time to listen to the Lord.

Ask Him – What do You want me to hear from you today? How do you want me to move towards You?

Lord, I exalt You for being so loving with me.
Thank you that Your love doesn't depend on how I act.
Forgive me for not loving others the way You do.
Thank You for delighting in me and desiring to be with me.
I ask for a loving heart that is gracious and kind. Amen.

REFLECTIONS

_____

_____

_____

_____

_____

_____

_____

_____

_____

_____

_____

_____

_____

_____

_____

_____

_____

_____

_____

_____

_____

_____

SESSION
FOUR

SESSION 4

DATE_____

CONVERSATION STARTERS

If you could plan a perfect vacation, what would it be?

What is the best advice you have ever received in your life?

What have your times with the Lord been like in the past few weeks?

How has God's love become real to you?

ENCOURAGEMENT STARTERS

Mentors, share about a time when God answered a seemingly impossible prayer.

Mentees, if you could ask your mentor one question today, what would it be?

PRAYER STARTERS

How can I pray for you today?

Look Up – Lord, I praise You for being my PEACE.

Peace I leave with you; my peace I give you. I do not give to you as the world gives. Do not let your hearts be troubled and do not be afraid. – John 14:27

May God himself, the God of peace, sanctify you through and through. May your whole spirit, soul and body be kept blameless at the coming of our Lord Jesus Christ. – 1 Thessalonians 5:23

God, I worship You for ...

Look Within – Lord, reveal to me if and where I may be letting anxiety, worry or fear rule in my life.

Look Around – Thank you, Lord, for these specific ways You have given me Your peace:

Look to Him – Father, these are the specific things I am asking and trusting You for:

A heart at peace gives life to the body. – Proverbs 14:30a

I pray that _____ will not be anxious about anything, but in every situation, by prayer and petition, with thanksgiving, _____ will present his/ her requests to God. And the peace of God, which transcends all understanding, will guard his/her heart and mind in Christ Jesus. – Philippians 4:6-7

Now, take time to listen to the Lord.

Ask Him – What do You want me to hear from You today? What do You want to teach me about Your peace?

God, I worship You for being the God of peace.
I confess my anxious thoughts that are focused on my circumstances and not on You.
Thank You for giving me a peace that actually guards my heart and mind.
I ask that you train my heart not to be anxious about anything but instead be more
prayerful and thankful. Amen.

∞

REFLECTIONS

SESSION
FIVE

SESSION 5

DATE_____

CONVERSATION STARTERS

When you look back on the past week, what amazes you the most?

What event or activity in the next few months are you looking forward to more than anything else?

What would you do for God if you knew you couldn't fail?

What is the most courageous thing you've ever done?

ENCOURAGEMENT STARTERS

Mentors, share a Scripture that you have been praying for your mentee.

Mentees, if you could ask your mentor one question today, what would it be?

PRAYER STARTERS

How can I pray for you today?

Look Up – God, I praise You for being my HOPE.

Guide me in your truth and teach me, for you are God my Savior, and my hope is in you all day long. – Psalm 25:5

"For I know the plans I have for you," declares the LORD, "plans to prosper you and not to harm you, plans to give you hope and a future." – Jeremiah 29:11

God, I love that You are ...

Look Within – Lord, open my eyes to see where I'm being negative about people or being hopeless about a circumstance.

Look Around – Father, thank You for these specific ways you have shown me Your goodness and given me hope.

Look to Him – Lord, I trust You and ask You to meet these specific needs in my life.

But those who hope in the LORD will renew their strength. They will soar on wings like eagles; they will run and not grow weary, they will walk and not be faint. – Isaiah 40:31

May the God of hope fill _____ with all joy and peace as he/she trusts in you, so that _____ may overflow with hope by the power of the Holy Spirit.
– Romans 15:13

Now, take time to listen to the Lord.

Ask Him – What do You want me to hear from You today? What Scripture passage do You want me to hold on to today? Where do You want me to have more hope?

God, I love that I can place my hope in You all day long.
I confess those times when I let hopelessness set in.
Thank You for filling me with all joy and peace as I trust in You.
I ask that my life will overflow with hope by the power of the Holy Spirit. Amen.

∽

REFLECTIONS

_____

_____

_____

_____

_____

_____

_____

_____

_____

_____

_____

_____

_____

_____

_____

_____

_____

_____

_____

_____

_____

_____

_____

∾

SESSION
SIX

SESSION 6

DATE_____

CONVERSATION STARTERS

Who is a famous person you would like to meet?

If you won $2 million tomorrow, what are the first three things you think you would do or buy as soon as you had the check in your hand?

What do you fear at this stage of your life?

What are you tempted to make into an idol?

ENCOURAGEMENT STARTERS

Mentors, share a struggle in your life where you have seen God help you overcome.

Mentees, what question would you like to ask your mentor this week?

PRAYER STARTERS

How can I pray for you today?

Look Up – Strong and mighty God, I praise You for being my DEFENDER.

A father to the fatherless, a defender of widows, is God in his holy dwelling.
– Psalm 68:5

For their Defender is strong; he will take up their case against you.
– Proverbs 23:11

Lord, the quality or attribute I appreciate about You is ...

Look Within – Lord, show me if I have a defensive attitude when I am criticized, confronted or rejected.

Look Around – Thank you, God, for these specific ways that You have protected and defended me.

Look to Him – God, as Your protected and defended one, I boldly ask You to provide for me in these ways.

Yet their Redeemer is strong; the LORD Almighty is his name. He will vigorously defend their cause so that he may bring rest to their land. – Jeremiah 50:34a

When _____ cries out to the LORD because of his/her oppressors, he will send _____ a savior and defender, and he will rescue him/her.
– Isaiah 19:20b

Now, take time to listen to the Lord.

Ask Him – Father, show me how and where I need to trust You to be my Defender. Reveal the places in my life that I need to trust You more.

Father, I praise You for being my Defender.
I confess any defensive attitude or critical spirit in my heart.
Thank You for being strong enough and wise enough to defend me with perfection.
I ask that You will bring rest to any situation in my life that is in turmoil. Amen.

REFLECTIONS

MID-
EVALUATION

MENTORING MID-EVALUATION

What do you like most about our mentoring relationship?

What could be improved to more effectively meet your needs?

In what ways is the mentoring experience different than you expected?

Would you make any changes to the way we meet (time, place, frequency, format, etc.)?

Any other suggestions for improvement?

SESSION
SEVEN

SESSION 7

DATE_____

CONVERSATION STARTERS

What is one item you own that you really should throw away but probably never will?

If you were to write a book, what would you choose as the subject?

Share a time when you felt cared for by God.

When you are sad, what helps you the most to make you feel better?

ENCOURAGEMENT STARTERS

Mentors, tell your mentee three great qualities that she has.

Mentees, tell your mentor something you appreciate about her.

PRAYER STARTERS

How can I pray for you today?

Look Up – Lord, I praise You for being my COMFORT.

Even though I walk through the darkest valley, I will fear no evil, for you are with me; your rod and your staff, they comfort me. – Psalm 23:4

Praise be to the God and Father of our Lord Jesus Christ, the Father of compassion and the God of all comfort, who comforts us in all our troubles, so that we can comfort those in any trouble with the comfort we ourselves receive from God. – 2 Corinthians 1:3-4

Lord, I exalt You for being ...

Look Within – Lord, make me aware of the times I don't comfort others in the way You comfort me.

Look Around – Thank you, God, for the specific ways you have been my comfort and shown me Your goodness.

Look to Him – Lord, give me wisdom and patience as I wait upon You. These are my specific requests.

For you know that we dealt with each of you as a father deals with his own children, encouraging, comforting and urging you to live lives worthy of God, who calls you into his kingdom and glory. – 1 Thessalonians 2:11-12

The LORD will surely comfort _____ and will look with compassion on all his/her ruins; he will make his/her deserts like Eden, his/her wastelands like the garden of the Lord. Joy and gladness will be found in _____, thanksgiving and the sound of singing. – Isaiah 51:3

Now, take time to listen to the Lord.

Ask Him – What do You want me to hear? What do You want me to apply from your Word?

Lord, I exalt You for being my Comfort when I am in the midst of trouble.
I confess those times when I don't comfort others the way You comfort me.
Thank You for understanding my emotions and for being so encouraging to me.
I ask that joy and gladness will be found in me in abundance. Amen.

∾

REFLECTIONS

SESSION
EIGHT

SESSION 8

DATE_____

CONVERSATION STARTERS

If you had no limitations, what would you like to do or where would you like to go?

What has brought a smile to your face today?

In what ways are you trusting the Lord that is beyond your capacity?

What is something the Holy Spirit is prompting you to do or say?

ENCOURAGEMENT STARTERS

Mentors, share a verse with your mentee that has been meaningful to you recently.

Mentees, what quality do you see in your mentor that you would like to emulate?

PRAYER STARTERS

How can I pray for you today?

Look Up – I praise You, God, for being my CONFIDENCE.

For you have been my hope, Sovereign LORD, my confidence since my youth.
– Psalm 71:5

Such confidence we have through Christ before God. Not that we are competent in ourselves to claim anything for ourselves, but our competence comes from God.
– 2 Corinthians 3:4-5

God, I worship You for Your ...

Look Within – Lord, reveal the sin of pride when I am overconfident or trusting myself more than You.

Look Around – Thank you, God, for how You have equipped me in these ways. Thank You for being my source for everything I need.

Look to Him – My God, help me rest in Your confidence in these specific areas of my life.

This is the confidence we have in approaching God: that if we ask anything according to his will, he hears us. – 1 John 5:14

Let _____ then approach the throne of grace with confidence, so that he/she may receive mercy and find grace to help him/her in his/her time of need. – Hebrews 4:16

Now, take time to listen to the Lord.

Ask Him – Lord, show me where my confidence is lacking or misplaced. What do You want to teach me about trust and placing my confidence in You?

God, I worship You for Your ability to be completely competent.
Forgive me for placing too much or too little confidence in myself.
Thank You that I can approach Your throne with confidence.
I ask that others will fully see that my confidence comes from You. Amen.

REFLECTIONS

SESSION
NINE

SESSION 9

DATE_____

CONVERSATION STARTERS

How would you describe today in just one word or phrase?

Name one thing that you think you do really well.

Is there an area of your life or an issue that needs to be surrendered to the Lord?

What is something you have done recently to make you feel closer to God?

ENCOURAGEMENT STARTERS

Mentors, share something you have learned recently from a book.

Mentees, share something specific that you have learned from your mentor.

PRAYER STARTERS

How can I pray for you today?

Look Up – Almighty God, I praise You for being my HELPER.

The LORD is my strength and my shield; my heart trusts in him, and he helps me. My heart leaps for joy, and with my song I praise him. – Psalm 28:7

So we say with confidence, "The LORD is my helper; I will not be afraid. What can man do to me?" – Hebrews 13:6

God, I love that You are ...

Look Within – Lord, show me areas in my life where I try to be self-sufficient and do not seek Your help.

Look Around – Thank you, God, for these specific ways You have helped me in the past and recently.

Look to Him – Holy God, I need Your help in these specific ways today.

LORD my God, I called to you for help and you healed me. – Psalm 30:2

So do not fear, for I am with you; do not be dismayed, for I am your God. I will strengthen _____ and help _____; I will uphold _____ with my righteous right hand. – Isaiah 41:10

Now, take time to listen to the Lord.

Ask Him – Father, what do You want to teach me? What promise do You want me to meditate on this week?

God, I love that You are always available to help me.
I confess my desire for self-sufficiency and thinking I can do it on my own.
Thank You for strengthening me and upholding me with Your righteous right hand.
I ask that You will help me not to fear but instead, call to You for help. Amen.

∞

REFLECTIONS

SESSION
TEN

SESSION 10

DATE_____

CONVERSATION STARTERS

Share about a time when you were surprised.

What would you order off the menu for your birthday?

Describe a time in the last several days when you felt the most (or least) free.

Who is someone in your life who is full of compassion?

ENCOURAGEMENT STARTERS

Mentors, tell your mentee three things you love about her.

Mentees, tell your mentor three things you love about her.

PRAYER STARTERS

How can I pray for you today?

Look Up – Precious Lord, I praise You for being full of COMPASSION.

Rend your heart and not your garments. Return to the LORD your God, for he is gracious and compassionate, slow to anger and abounding in love, and he relents from sending calamity. – Joel 2:13

The LORD is gracious and righteous; our God is full of compassion. – Psalm 116:5

Father, the quality or attribute I appreciate about You is ...

Look Within – Lord, I confess that I have not been very loving towards ...

Look Around – Thank you, Lord, for showing compassion to me. Make me aware of Your compassion in these areas of my life.

Look to Him – Father God, make my heart like Yours, eager to show compassion to these people in my life.

Be kind and compassionate to one another, forgiving each other, just as in Christ God forgave you. – Ephesians 4:32

I will strengthen _____ and save the tribes of _____. I will restore them because I have compassion on them. They will be as though I had not rejected them, for I am the LORD their God and I will answer them. – Zechariah 10:6

Now, take time to listen to the Lord.

Ask Him – Father, make me aware of those who need compassion. What do You want me to do with this awareness? Give me a willing heart to follow Your lead.

Father, I praise You for being so gracious and compassionate.
Lord, I confess my lack of grace towards others.
Thank You that Your compassions never fail. They are new every morning.
I ask for a heart of compassion and that I will see others the way You see them. Amen.

∾

REFLECTIONS

_____

_____

_____

_____

_____

_____

_____

_____

_____

_____

_____

_____

_____

_____

_____

_____

_____

_____

_____

_____

_____

SESSION
ELEVEN

SESSION 11

DATE_____

CONVERSATION STARTERS

What do you miss most about your childhood?

What is something dangerous or risky that you have always wanted to do?

Tell about a time when you heard God's voice speaking specifically to you.

Share an instance of losing your patience recently. How did others respond?

ENCOURAGEMENT STARTERS

Mentors, share with your mentee about a difficult relationship you have had and what God has taught you in the midst of it.

Mentees, tell your mentor something she has shared that has really changed your perspective.

PRAYER STARTERS

How can I pray for you today?

Look Up – Father God, I praise You for being PATIENT.

The Lord is not slow in keeping his promise, as some understand slowness. Instead he is patient with you, not wanting anyone to perish, but everyone to come to repentance.
– 2 Peter 3:9

But for that very reason I was shown mercy so that in me, the worst of sinners, Christ Jesus might display his immense patience as an example for those who would believe in him and receive eternal life. – 1 Timothy 1:16

Lord, I exalt You for being ...

Look Within – Father, give me insight to see the times that I have become impatient and not waited on You for Your perfect timing.

Look Around – Thank you, Father, for being immensely patient with me in these areas of my life.

Look to Him – Patient Lord, make me more like You. Reveal places in my life where You want me to learn to be more patient.

Be completely humble and gentle; be patient, bearing with one another in love.
– Ephesians 4:2

May _____ be joyful in hope, patient in affliction, faithful in prayer.
– Romans 12:12

Now, take time to listen to the Lord.

Ask Him – Remind me, Father, of the patience and mercy You have shown me. What do You want me to do differently to be more conformed to Your image?

Lord, I exalt You for being patient with me.
I confess my sin of impatience and rushing ahead without seeking You first.
Thank You for not giving up on me and for giving me second chances.
I ask for great patience as I wait on You to work out Your perfect will in my circumstances.
Amen.

REFLECTIONS

_____
_____
_____
_____
_____
_____
_____
_____
_____
_____
_____
_____
_____
_____
_____
_____
_____
_____
_____
_____
_____
_____
_____
_____
_____

SESSION
TWELVE

SESSION 12

DATE_____

CONVERSATION STARTERS

What is your least favorite household chore?

What is your favorite time of day and why?

Tell about a time when God provided immeasurably more than what you had asked for.

Share what this mentoring relationship has meant to you over the past 12 sessions.

ENCOURAGEMENT STARTERS

Both mentor and mentee, share one or two significant things God has taught you over the course of this time together.

PRAYER STARTERS

How can I pray for you today?

Look Up – Mighty and powerful God, I praise You for being my PROVIDER.

Command those who are rich in this present world not to be arrogant nor to put their hope in wealth, which is so uncertain, but to put their hope in God, who richly provides us with everything for our enjoyment. – 1 Timothy 6:17

He provides food for those who fear him; he remembers his covenant forever. – Psalm 111:5

God, I worship You for Your ...

Look Within – Lord, I confess my complaining or critical spirit when I'm not seeing Your provision.

Look Around – God, thank You for all the ways You provide for me, but specifically for Your provision in my past, how You are providing for me presently, and how You will provide for my future.

Look to Him – Lord, I ask You to help me recognize Your provision in all its various forms. I trust You to provide for this situation:

You gave abundant showers, O God; you refreshed your weary inheritance. Your people settled in it, and from your bounty, God, you provided for the poor. – Psalm 68:9-10

If _____ speaks, he/she should do so as one who speaks the very words of God. If _____ serves, he/she should do so with the strength God provides, so that in all things God may be praised through Jesus Christ. To him be the glory and the power for ever and ever. Amen. – 1 Peter 4:11

Now, take time to listen to the Lord.

Ask Him – Father, show me how and where I need to trust You to be my Provider. Show me what truth You want me to receive and hold onto forever.

God, I worship You for Your ability to richly provide for my every need.
I admit and acknowledge that I often complain and am not grateful for Your provision.
Thank You for knowing exactly what is best for me.
I ask that when You abundantly provide for me that I will always give You the glory.
Amen.

∞

REFLECTIONS

_____

_____

_____

_____

_____

_____

_____

_____

_____

_____

_____

_____

_____

_____

_____

_____

_____

_____

_____

_____

_____

PERSONAL
SUMMARY

PERSONAL SUMMARY

In what ways has the mentoring experience affected your relationship with the Lord and with others?

Which session had the most profound impact on your life and why?

Did any parts of the mentoring experience seem challenging or overwhelming to you?

What about the mentoring experience would lead you to suggest it to others?

If you could change something about the mentoring experience, what would you do differently?

How would you like to move forward? (Continue mentoring? Move on? Become a mentor to someone else? Other?)

COME. BE. MOVE.

Lord, here I am. I want to be all you have created me to be.
Now, move me to ...

_____

_____

_____

_____

_____

_____

_____

_____

_____

_____

_____

_____

_____

_____

_____

_____

_____

_____

_____

_____

_____

∽

Glorify the Lord with me; let us exalt his name together.

– Psalm 34:3

ACKNOWLEDGEMENTS

The book you hold in your hands has been in process for several years. Without the help and support of so many dear friends, it would still be in my head roaming about and not on paper to be effectively and powerfully used. Each of you is an important part of *Together*, beautifully exemplifying coming together, being together and moving together. I don't have enough words to adequately say "thank you" but I sure will try.

God – I was on my face on the floor before most writing sessions, desperately pleading for Your help. You get all the glory for any good that comes from this book. My prayer has been that the breath of the Almighty would breathe upon every word and into every mentoring relationship that will be touched through this tool. All praise goes to You and You alone!

Mark – To my wise, discerning, steady companion who gives me freedom to dream and accepts me for who I am. Thank you for faithfully walking alongside me, making me laugh like no other and for doing life together with me. I would choose you all over again.

Jess, Ben, Kati, and Matt – My dream as a little girl was to be a mom and you have made that dream come true. I might have a few more gray hairs because of the craziness that went on in our home in those early years, but it was so worth it. Thanks for giving me some good material to share with other moms. I have loved watching you grow into young adults who love the Lord. I absolutely love being your mom!

My Dear Friends – I'm forever grateful to all of you who have accompanied me and encouraged me on this journey of launching a ministry, writing a book, stepping out in faith and trusting God with every detail. With you by my side, I'm more courageous, confident, and full of hope. Thanks for continuing to point me to Jesus.

MORE Mentoring Team – Each one of you is so greatly loved and valued! Thank you, Jeannine, Kim, Michele, Val and Joy. You have beautiful, servant hearts and are willing to pour out your lives for kingdom purposes. I'm so thankful I don't have to do ministry alone. You make it much more fun doing it together!

My mentor, Fern Nichols – You have had a profound impact on my life. You're the kind of mom, wife, ministry leader, prayer warrior and friend who I want to model my life after. Thank you for investing in me so that I can invest in others.

My mentees – Thank you for letting me be me. You know all my issues and quirks and yet you love me just the same. I often feel like I'm being mentored more than I'm doing the mentoring. It's been a beautiful thing to watch – we truly are better together.

Toni Morse – You came along just when I needed you and I'm so thankful. Your finishing touches on the design and editing of this book were what got us through to the finish line. I will be forever grateful for the Lord connecting us in His perfect timing!

Prayer Team – To my prayer team of over 100 prayer warriors – thank you! We will never know on this side of heaven all of the specific ways God has moved because you have asked. Your prayers are the foundation of this ministry and will keep it going strong until we will be together in heaven. I can't wait for that celebration. Hopefully, our mansions will be in the same cul-de-sac!

Again, truly I tell you that if two of you on earth agree about anything they ask for, it will be done for them by my Father in heaven. For where two or three gather in my name, there am I with them.

– Matthew 18:19-20

TELL ME **MORE**

At MORE Mentoring, our vision is that every woman experiences MORE – more of Jesus, more fullness of life, more freedom and joy.

As a volunteer-powered non-profit ministry, we are devoted to **inspiring women to love and encourage others through prayer-focused mentoring.**

We care deeply about growing the local church by encouraging all women to be engaged in mentoring, whether as a mentor, a mentee, or both – because journeying together is better than going alone.

We come alongside churches, ministry leaders, and individuals to provide resources and tools for growing an effective mentoring movement and our dream is that mentoring becomes an integral part of every woman's life.

And to know this love that surpasses knowledge – that you may be filled to the measure of all the fullness of God. Now to him who is able to do immeasurably more than all we ask or imagine, according to his power that is at work within us, to him be glory in the church and in Christ Jesus throughout all generations, for ever and ever! Amen.

– Ephesians 3:19-21

morementoring.org
info@morementoring.org

SOCIALLY **MORE**

facebook.com/morementoring

instagram.com/morementoring

info@morementoring.org

morementoring.org
info@morementoring.org

IF YOU WANT **MORE**

TOGETHER MENTORING TOOLKIT

TOGETHER - An Online Course for Ministry Leaders is an affordable, easy, and convenient tool for ministry leaders who want mentoring to be a sought-after experience within the culture of their church or organization.

Available online: *morementoring.org*

TOGETHER - An Online Course for Mentors is an excellent way for any woman to learn how to be a truly effective mentor, someone well-equipped to love, listen, encourage, and pray.

Available online: *morementoring.org*

MORE MENTORING **RETREATS & EVENTS**

Check our schedule for upcoming retreats and events for groups and individuals

morementoring.org

morementoring.org
info@morementoring.org

ENDORSEMENTS

Bottom line for me? This skill is so important and often neglected — using Scripture to form the basis of shared and spoken prayer, including confession, between two or more believers. I love that this is a tool that can be used to train more women in the art of praying Scripture as well as mentoring. It is much needed (and desired!) from what I see and hear from Christian women in my sphere, mostly mothers with children still at home.
— LARA
Mentee, Colorado

MORE Mentoring has truly given our team just what we needed to get our church's mentoring ministry off the ground. From materials for use in mentoring sessions, application forms, and ongoing training calls throughout the year, they've helped make our year a great success. Nancy's encouragement, years of seasoned mentoring experience, and godly, wise counsel was just what we needed to put our team's vision of encouraging younger women in life and faith into place.
— VAL
Ministry Leader, Iowa

For quite some time, I have been trying to reconnect my heart and soul with God and get back to that daily quiet time to no avail. These 24 hours at the Come Away Retreat were just what I needed to get my spiritual life back on track. Thank you Nancy, MORE Mentoring, and sponsors. You have given me the gifts of refreshment, reconnection, dedication, and motivation!
— KIRSTEN
Attendee, Come Away Retreat

Mentoring has always been a life-giving and formative part of who I am and has now become an essential piece of how I live life. Being invited on a retreat with the opportunity of mentorship felt like God fanning into flame the call He's placed on my life. After being mentored for years, I feel equipped to step into the role of mentoring others.
— TARYN
Attendee, Come Away Retreat

∽

Made in the USA
Lexington, KY
03 December 2019

58001462R00057